the guide to owning a
Yorkshire Terrier

Elizabeth Downing

The Publisher wishes to acknowledge the following owners of the dogs in this book, including: Barnhill Yorkshire Terriers, Barbara Beissel, Leroy Chavez, Carol Confer, Wendy Garcia, Claudia Grunstra, Robert Harlow, Heskethane Yorkshire Terriers, Barbara Irwin, Nancy Kornick, Marie Larkin, Helen Melucci, Bonnie Myrick, Norman Odium, Dorothy Sims, Annabelle Tarman, and Melissa and Amy Zahralban.

T.F.H. Publications, Inc.
One TFH Plaza
Third and Union Avenues
Neptune City, NJ 07753

This book has been published with the intent to provide accurate and authoritative information in regard to the subject matter within. While every precaution has been taken in preparation of this book, the publisher and author assume no responsibility for errors or omissions. Neither is any liability assumed for damages resulting from the use of the information herein.

ISBN 0-7938-1862-1

www.tfh.com

Contents

The small and charismatic Yorkshire Terrier makes a wonderful companion for people of all ages.

History of the Yorkshire Terrier

The Yorkshire Terrier is one of the best-loved breeds of both the American and British dog-fancying public. His intelli-gence and courage are all out of proportion to his size. His good manners seem inherent, and his actions match his charming, elfin appearance. A wonderful friend and

A little dog with a lot of character, the independent Yorkie places little demand on his owner.

Most authorities agree that the Yorkie's origin can be traced to the continued mating of two related breeds: the Paisley Terrier and the Broken-Coated Scottish Terrier.

companion, he is also one of the most respected and sought-after of all dogs.

The proud owner of a Yorkshire Terrier has selected a pet that combines the sturdiness of terriers and the graciousness of Toy breeds! The diminutive Yorkie—small in size but large in character—has a surprisingly independent personality. He can amuse himself and makes few demands on his owner apart from grooming.

It is difficult to imagine a more desirable pet: he is a wonderful house-hold companion and, at the same time, one of the most accomplished of show breeds. Over one hundred years old, the Yorkshire Terrier is definitely a "man-made" breed. Yet the real source of his beginning is still in doubt. In Yorkshire, England, where the breed was first developed, the residents kept many terriers and Toy dogs as companions and, undoubtedly, many crosses were made among them. The same district also produced the Airedale, the largest of all terriers, and some authorities hold that the two breeds came from common parentage.

DEVELOPMENT

The original Yorkshire was by no means a toy. His weight ran from 12 to 14 pounds. The size has been reduced through selective breeding. Unlike other breeds that were developed by men of leisure, the Yorkshire Terrier was the dog of the common man.

Some of the dwarfing of the Yorkie's size was accomplished within 20 years of the time the dog first became recognized as a breed. For some time, the Yorkie did not breed true to type as far as weight was concerned, and specimens ranged from 2 3/4 to 13 pounds in the show ring! Even as late as 1880, when the Yorkie was introduced to American breeders, weights of the dogs were highly variable and unpredictable.

Most authorities agree that the development of the petite Yorkshire Terrier can be traced to the continued mating of two related breeds. The Paisley Terrier played a large part in the Yorkie's makeup. This extinct breed resembled the Skye Terrier in many respects, but the Paisley was shorter in the back. The Broken-Coated Scottish Terrier was also instrumental in the Yorkie's development. The mixture of the black and tan and white coat of this breed may account for the white sometimes found on the chest and paws of new-born Yorkshire puppies.

The first dogs to be prominently mentioned in connection with the Yorkshire Terrier's origin were Swift's Old Crab and Kershaw's Old Kitty. The former was a black and tan terrier from Manchester, and the latter was a blue terrier of the drop-ear Skye type. Huddersfield Ben, the first pillar of the Yorkshire breed, was the result of the mating of Old Crab and Old Kitty in 1850. A very potent sire, Huddersfield Ben transmitted his good qualities to his numerous progeny to a great

degree, and he is largely responsible for the appearance of the modern Yorkshire Terrier.

These little dogs were not always known as Yorkshire Terriers. They were first shown in England under the classification of "Broken-Coated Scottish or Yorkshire Terriers." About 1870, Mozart, a son of Huddersfield Ben, won a first prize in the Variety Class at the Westmorland show and a reporter commented that "they ought no longer to be called Scottish Terriers but Yorkshire Terriers." The name was an immediate success and subsequently caught on and was adopted.

Even the Yorkie's coat has undergone an evolution. Writing in 1857, in

Yorkies were first shown in England under the classification of "Broken-Coated Scottish or Yorkshire Terriers."

The Yorkshire Terrier is best known for his loyalty and courage.

the third edition of Dogs of the British Isles, Stonehedge said: "Since the first edition of this book was published, a considerable change has taken place in the type of several of the terrier family. At that time, the Yorkshire Terrier was represented by an animal only slightly differing from the old Scottish dog; his shape being nearly or exactly the same, and his coat differing simply in being more silky. Such an animal was Bounce (a champion of that day), and by comparing his portrait with that of Huddersfield Ben, it will readily be seen that a great development of coat has been accomplished in the latter."

NOTABLE YORKIES

It has become a matter of pride for breeders to advance well-researched theories of a dog's background; and no matter how hot the debate may wax, all agree that since emerging as a recognized breed, the Yorkshire Terrier has been notable for courage, loyalty, and stead-fastness. Greyfriars Bobby, who lived in Great Britain during the late 1800's, is a good example. Bobby was of the same root stock as our Yorkie, and they share a common ancestry.

No history of the Yorkshire Terrier would be complete without including the story of Smokey, a purebred Yorkie that was found in a shell hole after an American charge into Japanese lines in the New Guinea jungle. Smokey became the dog of soldier William

Although the Yorkie is primarily a house pet, he does enjoy spending time outdoors.

Wynne and went through 150 air raids, flew 12 air-sea rescue missions, and weathered a typhoon at Okinawa. Wynne, who had no previous experience in training dogs, taught her how to waltz, walk a tightrope, and jump through hoops. At Lingayen, the Signal Corps had to lay a telegraph wire through a 9-inch pipe under an airstrip. Smokey crawled 70 feet through the pipe, dragging a tow line attached to the wire. In her special parachute, Smokey learned how to make jumps from a 30-foot tower. She also ate C-rations and Spam, took soldiers' vitamin pills, and was bathed in Wynne's helmet.

The Standard for the Yorkshire Terrier

Of all the Toy breeds, there is no finer pet than the Yorkshire Terrier! He is small and sturdy, very lovable, and absolutely fearless.

The Yorkshire Terrier differs from other Toy breeds in one important and enviable quality: his extraordinarily

The mild-mannered Yorkie gets along easily with anyone, especially children.

fine temperament. He is calm and even-tempered and has a sunny disposition at all times. Never nervous or finicky, the Yorkie is one of the most amiable and contented, yet active, dogs known. He is not a one-man dog but shows affection to all in equal and generous measure—an ideal trait in any household pet but especially welcome when there are small children in evidence.

Perhaps the frosting on the cake is that the perfectly groomed Yorkie show dog is one of the most beautiful sights that a dog fancier can encounter. The best known characteristic of this handsome breed is a long, silky, and perfectly straight coat. In color, the Yorkshire Terrier is a beautiful steel blue from the tip of his head to the root of his tail, a rich golden tan on his head, and a bright tan on his chest, legs, and underparts.

It is an impressive spectacle to watch the tiny dog parade around the show ring, his small, delicate feet stepping sharp and his luxurious tail held high.

STANDARD FOR THE YORKSHIRE TERRIER

General Appearance—That of a long-haired toy terrier whose blue and tan coat is parted on the face and from the base of the skull to the end of the tail and hangs evenly and quite straight down each side of the body. The body is neat, compact and well proportioned. The dog's high head carriage and confident manner should give the appearance of vigor and self-importance.

Head—Small and rather flat on top, *the skull* not too prominent or round, *the muzzle* not too long, with **the bite** neither undershot nor overshot and teeth sound. Either scissors bite or level bite is acceptable. *The nose* is black. **Eyes** are medium in size and not too prominent; dark in color and sparkling with a sharp, intelligent expression. Eye rims are dark. **Ears** are small, V-shaped, carried erect and set not too far apart.

Body—Well proportioned and very compact. The back is rather short, the back line level, with height at the shoulder the same as at the rump.

Legs and Feet—*Forelegs* should be straight, elbows neither in nor out. *Hind legs* straight when viewed from behind, but stifles are moderately

According to the breed standard, the ideal Yorkie should have dark eyes that exude a warm and intelligent expression.

bent when viewed from the sides. *Feet* are round with black toenails. Dewclaws, if any, are generally removed from the hind legs. Dewclaws on the forelegs may be removed.

Tail—Docked to a medium length and carried slightly higher than the level of the back.

Coat—Quality, texture and quantity of coat are of prime importance. Hair is glossy, fine and silky in texture. Coat on the body is moderately long and perfectly straight (not wavy). It may be trimmed to floor length to give ease of movement and a neater appearance, if desired. The fall on the head is long,

Small, v-shaped, and
carried erect

Small and held high

Dark and medium in size

Black in color

Not too long

Round with black
toenails

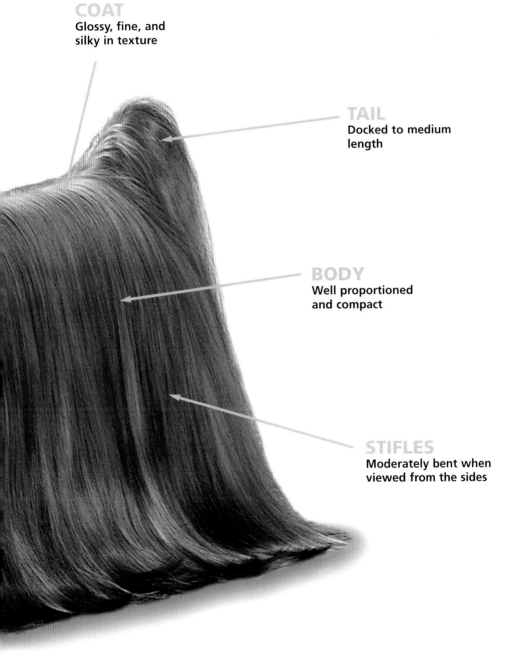

COAT
Glossy, fine, and silky in texture

TAIL
Docked to medium length

BODY
Well proportioned and compact

STIFLES
Moderately bent when viewed from the sides

The Yorkie's small, v-shaped ears stand upright and are set fairly close together.

The Yorkie's luxurious black and tan coat is one of his most distinctive characteristics.

tied with one bow in center of head or parted in the middle and tied with two bows. Hair on muzzle is very long. Hair should be trimmed short on tips of ears and may be trimmed on feet to give them a neat appearance.

Colors—Puppies are born black and tan and are normally darker in body color, showing an intermingling of black hair in the tan until they are matured. Color of hair on body and richness of tan on head and legs are of prime importance in *adult dogs*, to which the following color requirements apply:

BLUE: Is a dark steel-blue, not a silver blue and not mingled with fawn, bronzy or black hairs.

TAN: All tan hair is darker at the roots than in the middle, shading to still lighter tan at the tips. There should be no sooty or black hair intermingled with any of the tan.

Color on Body—The blue extends over the body from back of neck to root of tail. Hair on tail is darker blue, especially at end of tail.

Headfall—A rich golden tan, deeper in color at sides of head, at ear roots and on the muzzle, with ears a deep rich tan. Tan color should not extend down on back of neck.

Chest and Legs—A bright, rich tan, not extending above the elbow on the forelegs nor above the stifle on the hind legs.

Weight—Must not exceed seven pounds.

Approved April 12, 1966

Your New Yorkshire Terrier Puppy

SELECTION

When you pick out a Yorkshire Terrier puppy as a pet, don't be hasty; the longer you study puppies, the better you will understand them. Make it your trans-cendent concern to select a puppy that radiates good health and spirit and is lively on his feet. He should have bright eyes and a shiny coat, and he should come forward eagerly to make your acquaintance. Don't fall for any shy little darling that wants to retreat to his

Selecting the perfect puppy from an entire litter can be challenging. Choose the Yorkie puppy that best suits your personality.

When you purchase your Yorkie puppy, the breeder should supply you with the following important documents: a health certificate, inoculation records, the pedigree, a registration certificate, and a feeding schedule.

bed or his box, plays coyly behind other puppies or people, or hides his head under your arm or jacket appealing to your protective instinct. Pick the Yorkshire Terrier puppy that forthrightly picks you. The feeling of attraction should be mutual!

DOCUMENTS

Now, a little paperwork is in order. When you purchase a purebred Yorkshire Terrier puppy, you should receive a transfer of ownership, registration material, and other "papers" (a list of the immunization shots, if any, the puppy may have been given; a note on whether or not the puppy has been wormed; a

diet and feeding schedule to which the puppy is accustomed; etc.). Along with these documents, you are welcomed as a fellow owner to a long, pleasant association with a most lovable pet.

GENERAL PREPARATION

You have chosen to own a particular Yorkshire Terrier puppy. You have chosen him very carefully over all other breeds and all other puppies. So, before you have even gotten that adorable puppy home, you will have prepared for his arrival by reading everything you can get your hands on having to do with the management of the breed and the proper care of puppies. True, you will run into

Before purchasing a Yorkie, be aware of certain breed requirements, such as grooming needs.

When you get your Yorkie puppy, you will find that your reading and study are far from finished. You've just scratched the surface in your plan to provide the greatest possible comfort and health for him, and, by the same token, you do want to assure yourself of the greatest possible enjoyment of this wonderful creature. You must be ready for this puppy mentally, as well as physically.

TRANSPORTATION

If you take the puppy home by car, protect him from drafts, particularly in cold weather. Wrapped in a towel and carried in the arms or lap of a passenger, the Yorkshire Terrier puppy will usually make the trip without mishap. If the pup starts to drool and squirm, stop the car for a few minutes. Have newspapers handy in case of carsickness. A covered carton lined with newspapers provides protection for puppy and car, if you are driving alone. Avoid excitement and

many conflicting opinions, but at least you will not be starting "blind." Read, study, and digest. Talk over your plans with your veterinarian, other "Yorkshire Terrier people," and the breeder of your puppy.

Allow your Yorkie puppy enough time to eliminate before taking him home.

Yorkies make great playmates for children of all ages, provided they are both taught to respect and care for each other properly.

The bond between humans and animals, especially a lovable breed like the Yorkie, is a strong one. It's proven that pets help relieve stress and lessen the occurrence of illness in their owners.

Leaving the comfort of his mother and littermates can be difficult and frightening for a young puppy. Treat your Yorkie in a gentle and loving manner to ensure that he feels safe in his new environment.

unnecessary handling of the pup on arrival. A Yorkshire Terrier puppy is a very small "package" that will be making a complete change of surroundings and company, and he needs frequent rest and refreshment to renew his vitality.

THE FIRST DAY AND NIGHT

When your puppy arrives in your home, put him down on the floor and don't pick him up again, except when it is absolutely necessary. He is a dog, a real dog, and must not be lugged around like a rag doll. Handle him as little as possible, and permit no one to pick him up and baby him. Quite possibly, your Yorkshire Terrier puppy will be afraid in his new surroundings for a while, espe-

cially without his mother and littermates. Comfort him and reassure him, but don't console him. Don't give him the "oh-you-poor-itsy-bitsy-puppy" treatment. Be calm, friendly, and reassuring. Encourage him to walk around and sniff over his new home. If it's dark, put on the lights. Let him roam for a few minutes while you and everyone else concerned sit quietly or go about your routine business. Let the puppy come back to you.

Playmates may cause an immediate problem if the new Yorkshire Terrier puppy is to be greeted by children or other pets. If not, you can skip this subject. The natural affinity between puppies and children calls for some supervi-

Make your puppy's living area a comfortable, inviting place to which he can retreat and relax. These pups have decided to take over the laundry basket.

sion until a responsible relationship is established. This applies particularly to a "Christmas puppy," because this is a time when there is more excitement than usual and more chance for a puppy to experience something upsetting. It is a better plan to welcome the puppy several days before or after the holiday week. Like a baby, your Yorkshire Terrier puppy needs much rest and should not be over-handled. Once a child realizes that a puppy has "feelings" similar to his own and can readily be hurt or injured, the opportunities for play and responsibilities provide exercise and training for both child and pet.

For his first night with you, your pup should be placed where he is to sleep every night—say, in the kitchen, because the floor can usually be easily cleaned. Let him explore the area to his heart's content; close doors to confine him there. Prepare his food, and feed him lightly the first night. Give him a bowl with some water in it—not a lot, since most puppies will try to drink the whole bowl dry. Give him an old coat or shirt to lie on. Because a coat or shirt will be strong in human scent, the pup will pick it out to lie on, thus furthering his feeling of security in the room where he has just been fed.

HOUSETRAINING HELPS

Sooner or later—mostly sooner—your new Yorkshire Terrier puppy is going to "puddle" on the floor. First, take a newspaper and lay it on the puddle until the urine is soaked up onto the paper. Save this paper. Next, take a cloth with soap and water, wipe up the floor and dry it well. Then, take the wet paper and place it on a fairly large square of fresh newspapers in a convenient corner. When cleaning up, always keep a piece of wet paper on top of the others. Every time he wants to "squat," he will seek out this spot and use the papers. (This routine is rarely necessary for more than three days.) When you have done this, leave your Yorkshire Terrier puppy in his space for the night. Quite probably, he will cry and howl a bit; some are more stubborn than others on this matter. However, let him stay alone for the night. This may seem harsh treatment, but it is the best procedure in the long run. Just let him cry; he will soon weary of it.

THE GUIDE TO OWNING A YORKSHIRE TERRIER

Feeding Your Yorkshire Terrier

Let's talk about feeding your dog, a subject so simple that it's amazing there is so much nonsense and misunderstanding about it. Is it expensive to feed a Yorkshire Terrier? No, it is not! You can feed him economically and keep him in perfect shape the year round, or you can feed him expensive-

The amount of food a dog is fed depends on his age. For example, 4 small meals a day is sufficient for a 6-month-old Yorkie; 1 or 2 meals a day is sufficient for a 10- to 12-month-old dog.

A nutritious diet and daily exercise will keep your Yorkie in excellent physical condition.

ly. He'll thrive either way, so let's see why this is true.

First, remember that a Yorkshire Terrier is a dog. Dogs do not have a high degree of selectivity in their food, and unless you spoil them with great variety (and possibly turn them into poor, "picky" eaters), they will eat almost anything to which they become accustomed. Many dogs flatly refuse to eat nice, fresh beef. They pick around it and eat everything else. But meat—bah! Why? They aren't accustomed to it!

VARIETY IS NOT NECESSARY

A good general rule of thumb is: Forget about all human preferences and don't give a thought to variety. Choose the right diet for your Yorkshire Terrier and feed it to him day after day, year after year, winter and summer. But what is the right diet?

Hundreds of thousands of dollars have been spent in canine nutrition research. The results are pretty conclusive, so you needn't go into a lot of experimenting with trials of this and that every other week. Research has proven just what your dog needs to eat to stay healthy.

DOG FOOD

There are almost as many right diets as there are dog experts, but the basic diet most often recommended is one that consists of a dry food, either meal or kibble form. There are several of excellent quality, manufactured by reliable companies, research tested, and nationally advertised. They are inexpensive, highly satisfactory, and easily available in stores everywhere in containers of 5 to 50 pounds. Larger amounts cost less per pound, usually.

If you have a choice of brands, it is usually safer to choose the better known one; but even so, carefully read the analysis on the package. Do not choose any food in which the protein level is less than 25 percent, and be sure that this protein comes from both animal and vegetable sources. The good dog foods have meat meal, fish meal, liver, and such, plus protein from alfalfa and soybeans, as well as some dried-milk product. Note the vitamin content carefully. See that they are all there in good proportions; and be especially certain that the food contains properly high levels of vitamins A and D, two of the most perishable and important ones. Note the B-complex level, but don't worry about carbohydrate and mineral levels. These substances are plentiful and cheap and not likely to be lacking in a good brand.

The advice given for how to choose a dry food also applies to moist or canned types of dog foods, if you decide to feed one of these.

Having chosen a really good food, feed it to your Yorkshire Terrier as the manufacturer directs. Once you've started, stick to it. Never change your dog's diet if you can possibly help it. A switch from one meal or kibble-type food can usually be made without too much upset; however, a change will

A balanced diet is the foundation of your puppy's good health. Feeding him a quality brand of dog food will help him grow into a strong, sound adult.

If you are unsure about what type of diet is best for your Yorkie, consult your veterinarian.

almost invariably give you (and your Yorkshire Terrier) some trouble.

WHEN SUPPLEMENTS ARE NEEDED

Now, what about supplements of various kinds, mineral and vitamin, or the various oils? They are all okay to add to your Yorkshire Terrier's food. However, if you are feeding your dog a correct diet, and this is easy to do, no supplements are necessary unless your dog has been improperly fed, has been sick, or is having puppies. Vitamins and minerals are naturally present in all the foods; and to ensure against any loss through processing, they are added in concentrated form to the dog food you use. Except on the advice of your veterinarian, added amounts of vitamins can prove harmful to your Yorkie! The same risk applies to minerals.

FEEDING SCHEDULE

When and how much food do you give your Yorkshire Terrier? As to when (except in the instance of puppies), suit yourself. You may feed two meals per day or the same amount in one single feeding, either morning or night. As to how to prepare the food and how much to give, it is generally best to follow the directions on the food package. Your own Yorkshire Terrier may want a little more or a little less.

Fresh, cool water should always be available to your dog. This is important to good health throughout his lifetime.

ALL DOGS NEED TO CHEW

Puppies need something with resistance to chew on while their teeth and jaws are developing—for cutting the puppy teeth, to induce growth of the permanent teeth under the puppy teeth, to assist in getting rid of the puppy teeth at the proper time, to help the permanent teeth through the gums, to ensure normal jaw development, and to settle the permanent teeth solidly in the jaws.

The adult Yorkshire Terrier's desire to chew stems from the instinct for tooth cleaning, gum massage, and jaw exercise—plus the need for an outlet for periodic doggie tensions.

Feed your Yorkie a well-balanced, nutritious diet that includes the necessary amounts of proteins, carbohydrates, fats, minerals, and vitamins.

If you must leave your Yorkie unattended, he should be left in his crate to keep him out of trouble. A Nylabone® Fold-Away Pet Carrier is ideal.

Providing your Yorkie with safe, durable chew toys, like Nylabones®, will keep his jaw occupied and prevent him from chewing on the furniture.

This instinct is why dogs, especially puppies and young dogs, will often destroy property worth hundreds of dollars when their chewing instinct is not diverted from their owner's possessions. This is also why you should provide your Yorkie with something to chew—something that has the necessary functional qualities, is desirable from the dog's viewpoint, and is safe for him.

It is very important that your Yorkshire Terrier not be permitted to chew on anything he can break or on any indigestible thing from which he can bite sizable chunks. Sharp pieces, such as from a bone that can be broken by a dog, may pierce the intestinal wall and kill. Indigestible things that can be bitten off in chunks, such as from shoes or rubber or plastic toys, may cause an intestinal stoppage (if not regurgitated) and bring painful death, unless surgery is promptly performed.

Strong natural bones, such as 4- to 8-inch lengths of round shin bone from mature beef—either the kind you can get from a butcher or one of the variety available commercially in pet stores—may serve your dog's teething needs if

Training your Yorkie to practice proper chewing habits as a puppy will promote healthier teeth throughout his life. Supply safe chew toys, such as those made by Nylabone®.

his mouth is large enough to handle them effectively. You may be tempted to give your puppy a smaller bone and he may not be able to break it when you do, but puppies grow rapidly and the power of their jaws constantly increases until maturity. This means that a growing dog may break one of the smaller bones at any time, swallow the pieces, and die painfully before you realize what is wrong.

All hard natural bones are very abrasive. If your dog is an avid chewer, natural bones may wear away his teeth prematurely; hence, they then should be taken away from your dog when the teething purposes have been served. The badly worn, and usually painful, teeth of many mature dogs can be traced to excessive chewing on natural bones.

Contrary to popular belief, knuckle bones that can be chewed up and swallowed by your dog provide little, if any, usable calcium or other nutriment. They do, however, disturb the digestion of most dogs and cause them to vomit the nourishing food they need.

Dried rawhide products of various types, shapes, sizes, and prices are available on the market and have become quite popular. However, they don't serve the primary chewing functions very well; they are a bit messy when wet from mouthing, and most dogs chew them up rather rapidly—but they have been considered safe for dogs until recently. Now, more and more incidents of death, and near death, by strangulation have been reported to be the results of partially swallowed chunks of rawhide swelling in the throat. More recently, some veterinarians have been attributing cases of acute constipation to large pieces of incompletely digested rawhide in the intestine.

A new product, molded rawhide, is very safe. During the process, the rawhide is melted and then injection molded into the familiar dog shape. It is very hard and is eagerly accepted by dogs. The melting process also sterilizes the rawhide. Don't confuse this with pressed rawhide, which is nothing more than small strips of rawhide squeezed together.

The nylon bones, especially those with natural meat and bone fractions added, are probably the most complete, safe, and economical answer to

Taking proper care of your Yorkie's teeth will keep them free of tartar, help fight bad breath, and prevent gum disease.

There are many factors that contribute to a pet's happiness and well-being, such as a healthy living environment, good care, and unconditional love.

Nylafloss® helps to keep your Yorkie's teeth clean each time he chews on it.

the chewing need. Dogs cannot break them or bite off sizable chunks; hence, they are completely safe, and being longer lasting than other things offered for the purpose, they are economical. Nylabone® is highly recommended by veterinarians as a safe, healthy nylon bone.

Hard chewing raises little bristle-like projections on the surface of the nylon bones—to provide effective interim tooth cleaning and vigorous gum massage, much in the same way your toothbrush does it for you. The little projections are raked off and swallowed in the form of thin shavings, but the chemistry of the nylon is such that they break down in the stomach fluids and pass through without effect.

The toughness of the nylon provides the strong chewing resistance needed for important jaw exercise and effectively aids teething functions, but there is no tooth wear because nylon is nonabrasive. Being inert, nylon does not support the growth of microorganisms; and it can be washed in soap and water or it can be sterilized by boiling or in an autoclave.

Nothing, however, substitutes for periodic professional attention for your Yorkshire Terrier's teeth and gums, not any more than your toothbrush can do that for you. Have your dog's teeth cleaned at least once a year by your veterinarian (twice a year is better), and he will be happier, healthier, and a far more pleasant companion.

Grooming Your Yorkshire Terrier

BRUSHING

Daily brushing is a task that both you and your Yorkshire Terrier will enjoy. Your pet's clean coat and healthy sheen will be a source of pride for you—and surpris- ingly enough, your Yorkie will seem to prance more proudly himself! Your pet will enjoy the feeling of being fresh and clean. Brushing will give him a pleasant tingling sensation and will stimulate

Clipping your Yorkie's nails on a regular basis will add to his overall appearance. Be careful not to cut into the quick, because it will cause the nail to bleed.

A shiny coat is an indication that your Yorkie is in good health.

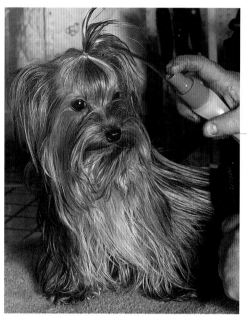

Before brushing your Yorkie's coat, spray it with coat dressing, which adds moisture and prevents hair breakage.

A thorough brushing involves three steps: (1) brush with the growth of the hair to clean the surface coat; (2) brush stiffly against the hair to clean the undercoat and massage the skin; (3) brush the hair back to its original position. These are the mechanics of brushing—a touch of loving care is the only added ingredient needed to make daily brushing fun and pleasant.

The ears should be scissored at the tips to where the ear begins to widen. Ears should be left quite clean. Part the hair from the base of the skull to the base of the tail, and brush down on either side with a bristle brush. Part the hair on the head at eye level from the corner of the eye to the top inside of the ear, pull upward and tie with a ribbon or barrette. Brush the fall (the long hair fringes on the face) downward.

the flow of oil in his skin. He will appreciate being free of nettles, and you will appreciate seeing the healthy hair that brushing promotes.

Wrapping your Yorkie's coat in wax paper or silk strips will encourage hair growth and is mostly used to develop a show coat.

Regularly brushing your Yorkie's coat will keep it clean, odor-free, and healthy.

Trim the feet with scissors following the outline of the paw, and trim the long flowing hairs enough to even them along the bottom. The hair of the coat should touch the ground. All in all, the Yorkie should have a "rectangular" appearance.

Hair growth can be encouraged by wrapping it in wax paper or strips of silk. This is done to develop a show coat. Section off small locks of hair, apply a small amount of baby oil, and fold each individual lock in a strip of paper or silk, securing it with a rubber band. These wrappings should not be left on for more than two or three days. Use a hair dressing or a spray to complete the grooming.

Carefully tended, the coat often sweeps the ground, but some fanciers choose to keep it slightly shorter. No matter what its length, the coat must be perfectly straight and of a fine silky texture. The keeping of a Yorkshire Terrier in "show shape" requires constant care, and it is necessary to start grooming the puppy at the age of three months, while his coat is still undeveloped. Accustom your young dog to standing on a table for his grooming sessions. If you break him in properly, he will not mind being handled and groomed later. The coat should be brushed every day with a soft bristle brush. Before brushing, spray the coat with a little coat dressing as the hairs are brittle when dry and may have a tendency to break. Pet shops also have a heavy oil that is excellent for keeping the Yorkie's hair from matting, or if some mats develop, they can be brushed out when impregnated with this oil.

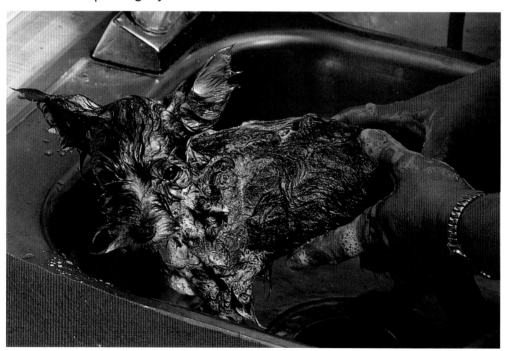

Be very careful not to get water in your Yorkie's eyes when bathing him.

Regular grooming sessions combined with an all-over body check will help you to stay on top of your dog's physical condition.

Normal brushing and care will give your Yorkie a good coat even if you do not go to the extreme of wrapping his hairs, but for a show dog this is a "must." Unlike most other breeds, the Yorkie requires frequent bathing—at least twice a month—but be sure to use a shampoo with a lanolin base as the bathings will otherwise dry out his coat and remove the oils from the skin.

BATHING

When you bathe your Yorkie choose a warm place and use several inches of warm water in a fairly deep tub. You will need a washcloth, dog soap or shampoo, and several terry cloth towels. Wash your pet's head and ears first, using a damp washcloth and no shampoo. Then wash him from front to back and top to bottom using circular strokes and working up plenty of suds. Care should be taken to keep your pet's eyes and ears free from soap. His skin and coat should be rinsed and dried thoroughly. One word of merry admonition—your Yorkshire Terrier's natural instinct is to shake himself dry, so don't take offense if you find yourself sharing his bath! Just blame yourself for not being quick enough with the towel.

When drying your Yorkie after his bath, be careful not to rub his coat vigorously; be gentle and pat the coat dry and then brush. You'll find it worthwhile to use a hair dryer to speed up drying after the bath. A

Untrimmed nails can spread and weaken your dog's feet. Trimming his nails every other week will keep them neat and strong.

THE GUIDE TO OWNING A YORKSHIRE TERRIER

dryer on a stand is best, although a portable dryer will do an effective job. The dryer not only reduces the possibility of your dog's catching a cold after a bath, but also helps keep his coat fluffy.

Daily brushing and bi-monthly bathing will help your Yorkie develop his coat. Never trim the Yorkie, but cut the hair on his ears as its weight may make his ears droop. You don't want him to look like a miniature Old English Sheep Dog, so keep the hair off his eyes by pulling it back and tying it in place with a ribbon or a rubber band topknot. The back should have a part in it running down the middle, and the hair should fall down straight on either side.

NAIL TRIMMING

As the Yorkie probably won't do too much running on rough ground, you'll have to have his toenails trimmed occasionally. You may accomplish this yourself and will need one, and possibly two, instruments to perform the task of nail trimming: a nail clipper is useful, and a fairly coarse file may be used to shape your pet's nails for show.

The important point to watch when attending to your pet's nails is not to cut into the quick. This is seen from any position in white nails, but in those nails that are black or dark in color it is more easily located from the underneath part of the nail where it has a soft, spongy appearance in contrast to the hard brittleness of the nail matter itself.

Immediately after bathing your Yorkie, wrap him in a towel and gently pat him dry.

When using a nail file, it should be drawn from the top of the nail downward in a round stroke to the end of the nail underneath. Considerable pressure is needed for the first few strokes in order to break through the hard polished surface of the nail. After the first few strokes the filing is easily accomplished.

Periodically, clean out your dog's ears with a cotton swab dipped in alcohol.

Yorkies may have problems with their teeth. Don't be alarmed if you find two sets of teeth in your puppy's mouth, as this happens sometimes. Have your vet extract the excess teeth so that the permanent teeth will grow in naturally and not be crooked. Yorkies' teeth often have a tendency to discolor, so have your vet check them whenever you have reason to visit.

Training Your Yorkshire Terrier

You owe your dog proper training. The privilege of being trained is his birthright. Whether your Yorkshire Terrier is going to be a handsome, well-mannered housedog and companion, a show dog, or a working dog, the basic training is always the same—all dogs must start with basic obedience, or what might be called "manners training."

Your dog must come instantly when called and obey the sit and down commands just as fast; he must walk

Allow your Yorkie to get the proper rest before training. You will get the best results when he is alert and motivated.

Teaching your Yorkie good manners and obedience skills will ensure that he will become a treasured member of the family for years to come.

A good way to reinforce basic training is to have your Yorkie perform simple commands, such as sit or down, before eating.

Praise and treats used in conjunction with the commands will help motivate your puppy to achieve the desired responses.

quietly at heel, whether on or off the lead. He must be mannerly and polite wherever he goes, on the street, and in stores. Your dog must be orderly in the presence of other dogs. He must not bark at children on roller skates, at motorcycles, or at other domestic animals. Also, he must be restrained from chasing cats; it is not a dog's inalienable right to chase cats, and he must be reprimanded for it.

PROFESSIONAL TRAINING

How do you go about this training? Well, it's a simple procedure, very standard-ized by now. First, if you can afford the extra expense, you may send your dog to a professional trainer, and in 30 to 60 days he will learn how to be "a good dog." If you enlist these professional services, follow the advice given about when to come to see your dog. No, he won't forget you, but frequent visits at the wrong time may slow down his training progress. In using a "pro" trainer, you will have to go for some training, too, after the trainer feels your dog is ready to go home. You will have to learn how your dog works, just what to expect of him, and how to use what he has learned after he is home.

OBEDIENCE TRAINING CLASS

Another way to train your dog (I think this is the best way) is to join an obedience training class right in your own area. There is such a group in nearly every community nowadays. In this class, you will be working with a group of people who are also just starting out. You will actually be training your own dog, since all work is under the direction of a head trainer who will make suggestions to you and also tell you when and how to correct your dog's errors. Your dog will also learn to get along with other dogs. More importantly, he will learn to do exactly what he is told to do, no matter how much confusion there is around him or how great the temptation to go his own way.

Training your Yorkie to walk on a leash will give you the chance to enjoy quality time outside together.

A well-socialized pet is able to get along with other people and animals, including birds.

Write to the American Kennel Club for the location of a training club or class in your locality. Sign up. Go to it regularly—every session! Go early and leave late! Both you and your dog will benefit tremendously.

TRAIN HIM BY THE BOOK

The third way of training your dog is by the book. Yes, you can do it this way, and do a good job of it, too. In using the book method, select a book, buy it, and study it carefully; then study it some more, until the procedures are almost second nature to you. Now, start your training. However, go by the book, and stick to its advice and exercises. Don't start in, and then make up a few rules of your own. If you don't follow the book, you'll get into jams you can't get out of

by yourself. If, after a few hours of short training sessions, your dog is still not working as he should, get back to the book for a study session, because it's *your* fault, not the dog's! The procedures of dog training have been so well systematized that it is probably your fault, because literally thousands of fine Yorkshire Terriers have been trained by the book.

After your Yorkie is "letter perfect" under all conditions, you may wish to go on to advanced training and trick work.

Your Yorkie will love his obedience training, and you'll burst with pride at the finished product! He will enjoy life even more, and you'll enjoy your dog more. And remember—you owe your dog good training.

THE GUIDE TO OWNING A YORKSHIRE TERRIER

Showing Your Yorkshire Terrier

A show dog is a comparatively rare thing. He is one dog out of several litters of puppies. He happens to be born with a degree of physical perfection that closely approximates the standard by which the breed is judged in the show ring. Such a dog should, on maturity, be able to win or approach his championship in good, fast company at the larger shows. Upon finishing his championship, he is apt to be as highly desirable as a breeding animal. As a proven stud, he will automatically command a high price for service.

Showing dogs is a lot of fun, but it is also a highly competitive sport. While all the experts were once beginners, the odds are against a novice. You will be showing against experienced handlers, often people who have devoted a lifetime to breeding, picking the right dogs, and then showing them through to their championships. Moreover, the most perfect dog ever born has faults, and in your hands the faults will be far more evident than with the experienced handler who knows how to minimize them. These are but a few points on the difficult side of the picture.

The experienced handler, as I say, was not born knowing the ropes. He learned—*and so can you!* You can succeed if you put in the same effort, study, and keen observation that he did. But it will take time!

KEY TO SUCCESS

First, search for a truly fine show prospect. Take the puppy home, raise him by the book, and as carefully as you know how, give him every chance to mature into the dog you hoped for. My advice is to keep your dog out of

Before you enter your Yorkie in competition, make sure that he adheres to the breed standard.

big shows, even Puppy Classes, until he is mature. Maturity in the male is roughly at two years of age; in the female, 14 months or so. When your dog is approaching maturity, start him out at match shows. With this experience, you can then go gunning for the big wins at the big shows.

Next, read the standard by which the breed is judged. Study it until you know it by heart. Having done this, and while your puppy is at home (where he should be) growing into a normal, healthy dog, attend every dog show you possibly can. Sit at the ringside and watch Yorkshire Terrier judging. Keep your ears and eyes open. Do your own judging, holding each of those dogs against the standard, which you now know inside out.

In your evaluations, don't start looking for faults. Look for the virtues—the best qualities. How does a given dog shape up against the standard? Having looked for and noted the virtues, then note the faults and see what prevents a given dog from standing correctly or moving well. Weigh these faults against the virtues, since, ideally, every feature of the dog should contribute to the harmonious whole dog.

Your Yorkie will provide you with many years of companionship if he receives the proper care and love from the start.

Proper grooming is essential to your Yorkie's success in the show ring.

RINGSIDE JUDGING

It's a good practice to make notes on each dog, always holding the dog against the standard. In "ringside judging," forget your personal preference for this or that feature. What does the standard say about it? Watch carefully as the judge places the dogs in a given class. From the ringside, it is sometimes difficult to see why number one was placed over the second dog. Try to follow the judge's reasoning. If possible, try to talk with him after judging is finished. Ask questions as to why he placed certain dogs and not others. Listen carefully while the judge explains his placings—I'll say right here, any judge worthy of his license should be able to give sound reasons.

When you're not at the ringside, talk with the fanciers who have Yorkshire Terriers. Don't be afraid to ask opinions or say that you don't know. It will help you a great deal and speed up your personal progress if you are a good listener.

THE NATIONAL CLUB

You will find it worthwhile to join the national Yorkshire Terrier club and to subscribe to its magazine. From the national breed club, you will learn the location of an approved regional club near you. When your young Yorkie is eight to ten months old, find out the dates of match shows in your section of the country. They differ from regular shows only in that no championship points are given. These shows are especially designed to launch young dogs (and new handlers) on a show career.

ENTER MATCH SHOWS

With the ring deportment you have watched at big shows firmly in mind and in practice, enter your dog in as many match shows as you can. In the ring, you have two jobs. One is to see to it that your dog is always being seen to his best advantage. The other job is to keep your eye on the judge to see what he may want you to do next. Watch only the judge and your dog. Be quick and be alert; do exactly as the judge directs. Don't speak to him except to answer his questions. If he does something you don't like, don't say so. Also, don't irritate the judge (and everybody else) by constantly talking and fussing with your dog.

In moving about the ring, remember to keep clear of dogs beside you or in front of you. It is my advice to you *not* to show your Yorkie in a regular point show until he is at least close to maturity and after both you and your dog have had time to perfect ring manners and poise in the match shows.

Your Healthy Yorkshire Terrier

Your Yorkshire Terrier is a prancing stat-uete of good health: a rich, vibrant blue/tan coat, clear eyes, pink gums, moist nose, and ever-alert and active. We know our pets, their moods and habits, and therefore we can recognize when our Yorkie is experiencing an off-day. Signs of sickness can be very obvi-

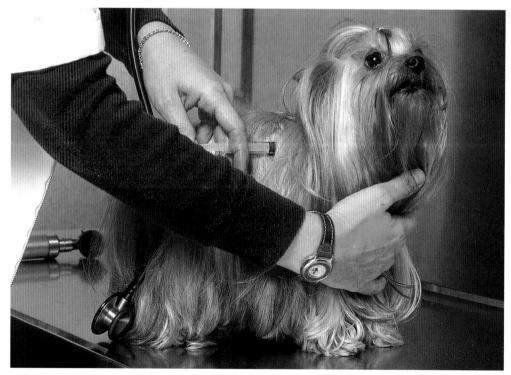

Maintaining your Yorkie's immunization schedule and booster shots will help him live a long and healthy life.

A shiny coat, clear bright eyes, and an energetic attitude are indications that your Yorkie is in good health.

Yorkies may be prone to certain eye diseases. Regular veterinary visits can help detect any health problems before becoming too serious.

ous or very subtle. As any mother can attest, diagnosing and treating an ailment requires common sense, knowing when to seek home remedies and when to visit your doctor, or veterinarian, as the case may be.

Your veterinarian is your Yorkshire Terrier's best friend, next to you. It will pay to be choosy about your veterinarian. Talk to dog owning friends whom you respect. Visit more than one vet before you make a lifelong choice. Trust your instincts. Find a knowledgeable, compassionate vet who knows Yorkshire Terriers and likes them.

MAJOR HEALTH ISSUES

Fortunately for Yorkie people (and the Yorkies themselves), very few breed-specific health concerns have arisen in the breed. The most prominent concerns affect the bones, including Legg-Calves-Perthes disease (LCP), slipped stifles, and patellar luxation. LCP occurs in small dogs from the age of four to 12 months and involves the hip joint, usually one leg only. The problem does not resolve itself, as is true with certain other diseases that affect the bones and joints of young dogs. Removal of the femur (knee cap) is the treatment of choice. Affected dogs experience lameness and pain as well as muscle atrophy.

Yorkies may be prone to certain eye problems including keratitis sicca and distichiasis. Breeders are screening eyes for possible problems in their lines, including progressive retinal atrophy (PRA). With PRA, blindness is the final result of the progressive impairment of vision. In the Yorkie, as in all breeds affected by this condition, it is believably inherited, though there are different varieties that affect each breed uniquely.

ANAL SACS

An owner must pay special attention to anal sacs, sometimes called anal glands, which are located in the musculature of the anal ring, one on either side. Each empties into the rectum via a small duct. Occasionally, their secretion becomes thickened and accumulates so you can readily feel these structures from the outside. If your Yorkshire Terrier is scooting across the floor dragging his rear quarters, or licking his rear, his anal sacs may need to be expressed. Placing pressure in and up toward the anus, while holding the tail, is the general routine. Anal sac secretions are characteristically foul-smelling, and you could get squirted if not careful. Veterinarians can take care of this during regular visits and demonstrate the cleanest method.

VACCINATIONS

For the continued health of your dog, owners must attend to vaccinations regularly. Your veterinarian can recommend a vaccination schedule appropriate for your dog, taking into consideration the factors of climate and geography. The basic vaccinations to protect your dog are: parvovirus, distemper, hepatitis, leptospirosis, adenovirus, parainfluenza, coronavirus, bordetella, tracheobronchitis (kennel cough), Lyme disease, and rabies.

Parvovirus is a highly contagious, dog-specific disease, first recognized in 1978. Targeting the small intestine, parvo affects the stomach, and diarrhea and vomiting (with blood) are clinical signs. Although the dog can pass the disease to other dogs within three days of infection, the initial signs, which include lethargy and depression, don't display themselves for four to seven days. When affecting puppies under four weeks of age, the heart muscle is frequently attacked. When the heart is affected, the puppies exhibit difficulty in breathing and experience crying and foaming at the nose and mouth.

Distemper, related to human measles, is an airborne virus that spreads in the blood and ultimately in the nervous system and epithelial tissues. Young dogs or dogs with weak immune systems can develop encephalomyelitis (brain disease) from the distemper infection. Such dogs experience seizures, general weakness and rigidity, as well as "hardpad." Since distemper is largely

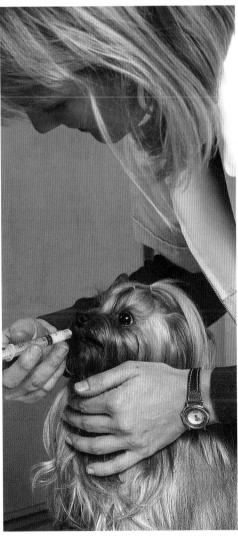

A young puppy is extremely vulnerable to diseases. Take special precautions to keep your Yorkie protected and healthy throughout his life.

Parasites can be transmitted to your puppy via other dogs. Make sure that your Yorkie has received the proper immunizations before taking him out to make new friends.

incurable, prevention through vaccination is vitally important. Puppies should be vaccinated at 6 to 8 weeks of age, with boosters at 10 to 12 weeks. Older puppies (16 weeks and older) that are unvaccinated should receive no fewer than two vaccinations at three to four week intervals.

Hepatitis mainly affects the liver and is caused by canine adenovirus type I. Highly infectious, hepatitis often affects dogs 9 to 12 months of age. Initially, the virus localizes in the dog's tonsils and then disperses to the liver, kidneys, and eyes. Generally speaking, the dog's immune system is capable of combating this virus. Canine infectious hepatitis affects dogs that have systems that cannot fight off the adenovirus. Affected

dogs have fever, abdominal pains, bruising on mucous membranes and gums, and experience coma and convulsions. Prevention of hepatitis exists only through vaccination at eight to ten weeks of age, boosters three or four weeks later, then annually.

Leptospirosis is a bacterium-related disease, often spread by rodents. The organisms that spread leptospirosis enter through the mucous membrane and spread to the internal organs via the bloodstream. It can be passed through the dog's urine. Leptospirosis does not affect young dogs as consistently as other viruses; it is reportedly regional in distribution and somewhat dependent on the immunostatus of the dog. Fever, inappetence, vomiting, dehydration, hemorrhage, and kidney and eye disease can result in moderate cases.

Bordetella, called canine cough, causes a persistent hacking cough in dogs and is very contagious. Bor-detella involves a virus and a bacteria: parainfluenza is the most common virus implicated; bordetella bronchiseptica, the bacterium. Bronchitis and pneumonia result in less than 20 percent of the cases, and most dogs recover from the condition within a week to four weeks. Nonprescription medicines can help relieve the hacking cough, though nothing can cure the condition before it's run its course. Vaccination cannot guarantee protection from canine cough, but it does ward off the most common virus responsible for the condition.

Lyme disease (also called borreliosis), although known about for decades, was only first diagnosed in dogs in 1984. Lyme disease can affect cats, cattle, and horses, but especially people. In the US, the disease is transmitted by two ticks carrying the *Borrelia burgdorferi* organism: the deer tick (*Ixodes scapularis*) and the western black-legged tick (*Ixodes pacificus*), the latter primarily affects reptiles. In Europe, *Ixodes ricinus* is responsible for spreading Lyme. The disease causes lameness, fever, joint swelling, inappetence, and lethargy. Removal of ticks from the dog's coat can help reduce the chances of Lyme, though not as much as avoiding heavily wooded areas where the dog is most likely to contract ticks. A vaccination is available, though it has not been proven to protect dogs from all strains of the organism that cause the disease.

Rabies is passed to dogs and people through wildlife—in North America, principally through the skunk, fox, and raccoon; the bat is not the culprit it was once thought to be. The common image of the rabid dog foaming at the mouth with every hair on end is unlikely the truest scenario. A rabid dog exhibits difficulty eating, salivates much, and has spells of paralysis and awkwardness. Before a dog reaches this final state, he may experience anxiety, personality changes, irritability, and more aggres-

Keeping your yard clean is the best prevention against worms. A fenced-in area is also helpful in keeping stray and potentially infected dogs away from your Yorkie.

siveness than is usual. Vaccinations are strongly recommended as affected dogs are too dangerous to manage and are commonly euthanized. Puppies are generally vaccinated at 12 weeks of age, and then annually. Although rabies is on the decline in the world community, tens of thousands of humans die each year from rabies-related incidents.

COPING WITH PARASITES

Parasites have clung to our pets for centuries. Despite our modern efforts, fleas still pester our pet's existence, and our own. All dogs itch, and fleas can make even the happiest dog a miserable, scabby mess. The loss of hair and habitual biting and chewing at themselves rank among the annoyances; the nuisances include the passing of tapeworms and the whole family itching through the summer months. A full range of flea-control and elimination products are available at pet shops, and your veterinarian surely has recommendations. Sprays, powders, collars, and dips fight fleas from the outside; drops and pills fight the good fight from inside. Discuss the possibilities with your vet. Not all products can be used in conjunction with one another, and some dogs may be more sensitive to certain applications than others. The dog's living quarters must be debugged as well as the dog himself. Heavy infestation may require multiple treatments.

Always check your dog for ticks well. Although fleas can be acquired almost anywhere, ticks are more likely to be picked up in heavily treed areas, pastures, or other outside grounds (such as dog shows or obedience or field trials). Athletic, active, and hunting dogs are the most likely subjects, though any passing dog can be the host. Remember, Lyme disease is passed by tick infestation.

There are many parasites, like fleas and ticks, that your Yorkie may encounter while playing outside. Check his coat thoroughly after he has been outdoors.

THE GUIDE TO OWNING A YORKSHIRE TERRIER

Yorkies enjoy spending time outdoors. Be sure to take every precaution to prevent your dog from becoming infested with parasites.

Young puppies should always be supervised when playing outdoors

As for internal parasites, worms are potentially dangerous for dogs and people. Roundworms, hookworms, whipworms, tapeworms, and heartworms comprise the blightsome party of troublemakers. Deworming puppies begins at around two to three weeks and continues until three months of age. Proper hygienic care of the environment is also important to prevent contamination with roundworm and hookworm eggs. Heartworm preventatives are recommended by most veterinarians, although there are some drawbacks to the regular introduction of poisons into our dogs' systems. These daily or monthly preparations also help regulate most other worms as well. Discuss worming procedures with your veterinarian.

Roundworms pose a great threat to dogs and people. They are found in the intestines of dogs, and can be passed to people through ingestion of feces-contaminated dirt. Roundworm infection can be prevented by not walking dogs in heavy-traffic people areas, by burning feces, and by curbing dogs in a responsible manner. (Of course, in most areas of the country, curbing dogs is the law.) Roundworms are typically passed from the bitch to the litter, and bitches should be treated along with the puppies, even if they tested negative prior to whelping. Generally, puppies are treated every two weeks until two months of age.

A happy and healthy Yorkie is a welcome addition to any household.

Hookworms, like roundworms, are also a danger to dogs and people. The hookworm parasite (known as *Ancylostoma caninum*) causes cutaneous larva migrans in people. The eggs of hookworms are passed in feces and become infective in shady, sandy areas. The larvae penetrate the skin of the dog, and the dog subsequently becomes infected. When swallowed, these parasites affect the intestines, lungs, windpipe, and the whole digestive system. Infected dogs suffer from anemia and lose large amounts of blood in the places where the worms latch onto the dog's intestines, etc.

Although infrequently passed to humans, whipworms are cited as one of the most common parasites in America. These elongated worms affect the intestines of the dog, where they latch on and cause colic upset or diarrhea. Unless identified in stools passed, whipworms are difficult to diagnose. Adult worms can be eliminated more consistently than the larvae, since whipworms live unusual life cycles. Proper hygienic care of outdoor grounds is critical to the avoidance of these harmful parasites.

Providing the proper health care for all of your pets will prevent them from passing on illnesses to one another.

Yorkies are loyal, affectionate dogs that make an excellent addition to any household. Be sure to give your pet all the love and care you can.

With the proper diet, grooming, and health care, your Yorkshire Terrier will be a lifelong companion.

Tapeworms are carried by fleas, and enter the dog when the dog swallows the flea. Humans can acquire tapeworms in the same way, though we are less likely to swallow fleas than dogs are. Recent studies have shown that certain rodents and other wild animals have been infected with tapeworms, and dogs can be affected by catching and/or eating these other animals. Of course, outdoor hunting dogs and terriers are more likely to be infected in this way than are your typical house dog or nonmotivated hound. Treatment for tapeworms has proven very effective, and infected dogs do not show great discomfort or symptoms. When people are infected, however, the liver can be seriously damaged. Proper cleanliness is the best bet against tapeworms.

Heartworm disease is transmitted by mosquitoes and badly affects the lungs, heart, and blood vessels of dogs. The larvae of *Dirofilaria immitis* enter the dog's bloodstream when bitten by an infected mosquito. The larvae take about six months to mature. Infected dogs suffer from weight loss, appetite loss, chronic coughing, and general fatigue. Not all affected dogs show signs of illness right away, and carrier dogs may be affected for years before clinical signs appear. Treatment of heartworm disease has been effective but can be dangerous also. Prevention, as always, is the desirable alternative. Ivermectin™ is the active ingredient in most heartworm preventatives and has proven to be successful. Check with your veterinarian for the preparation best for your dog. Dogs generally begin taking the preventatives at eight months of age, and continue to do so throughout the nonwinter months.

Index

Photo Credits

Karen Taylor, p. 28
All other photos by Isabelle Francais